M000036185

Junior
Classroom **Atlas**
4th Edition

Cartography
Gregory Babiak
Rob Ferry

Design Director
Joerg Metzner

Graphic Designer
Jennifer Stewart

Photo Credits
l = left, c = center, r = right, t = top, b = bottom
Cover: all ©istockphoto; p. 4 ©Lostutnikov/Shutterstock; p. 5 ©istockphoto; p. 7 ©istockphoto; p. 9 ©istockphoto; p. 10 t ©istockphoto, tc ©istockphoto, bc ©Jess Kraft/Shutterstock, b ©istockphoto; p. 11 ©istockphoto; p. 12 t ©Joyce Sherwin/Shutterstock, tc ©istockphoto, bc ©istockphoto, b ©istockphoto; p. 13 all ©istockphoto; p. 14 ©istockphoto; p. 16-17 all ©istockphoto; p. 18 ©istockphoto; p. 19 (timeline l to r) ©istockphoto, ©Everett Historical/Shutterstock, ©istockphoto, ©istockphoto, ©istockphoto; tl ©Tao Jiang/Shutterstock, tc ©istockphoto, tr ©istockphoto, cl ©istockphoto, c ©age fotostock/Alamy, cr ©istockphoto; p. 20 ©istockphoto; p. 21 (timeline l to r) ©Anton_Ivanov/Shutterstock, ©istockphoto, ©istockphoto, ©Hola Images/Alamy, ©istockphoto; tl ©Trent Townsend/Shutterstock, tr ©istockphoto, cl ©Fred Cardoso/Shutterstock, c ©Anton_Ivanov/Shutterstock, cr ©istockphoto; p. 23 ©istockphoto; p. 24-25 (timeline l to r) ©Tanjala Gica/Shutterstock, ©Nick Pavlakis/Shutterstock, ©mountainpix/Shutterstock, ©JeniFoto/Shutterstock, ©ndphoto/Shutterstock, ©Everett Historical/Shutterstock, ©BMCL/Shutterstock, ©timsimages/Shutterstock; p. 24 tl ©barbar34/Shutterstock, tr ©beboy/Shutterstock, cl ©Fedor Selivanov/Shutterstock, cr ©S. Borisov/Shutterstock; p. 25 tl ©Lenar Musin/Shutterstock, tr ©istockphoto, cl ©istockphoto, c ©Mikhailo/Shutterstock, cr ©mRGB/Shutterstock; p. 26 ©istockphoto; p. 27 (timeline l to r) ©istockphoto, ©istockphoto, ©Anders Blomqvist/Lonely Planet Images, ©Milana Tkachenko/Shutterstock, ©istockphoto, ©yui/Shutterstock; tl ©istockphoto, cl ©istockphoto, c ©istockphoto, cl ©istockphoto; p. 29 ©istockphoto; p 30-31 (timeline all) ©istockphoto; p. 30 tl ©istockphoto, tc ©istockphoto, tr ©istockphoto, cl ©Everything/Shutterstock, c ©istockphoto, cr ©istockphoto; p. 31 all ©istockphoto; p. 32 ©istockphoto; p. 33 (timeline l to r) ©Sasapee/Shutterstock, ©f9photos/Shutterstock, ©istockphoto, ©istockphoto, ©istockphoto; tl ©Natalia Fadosova/Shutterstock, tr ©istockphoto, cl ©Stanilav Fosenbauer/Shutterstock, c ©Jason Ho/Shutterstock, cr ©Brian Kinney/Shutterstock; p. 34 ©istockphoto; p. 35 (timeline l to r) ©Denis Burdin/Shutterstock, ©f9photos/Shutterstock, ©I. Noyan Yilmaz/Shutterstock; tc ©istockphoto, tr ©Anton_Ivanov/Shutterstock, cl ©Footage.Pro/Shutterstock, c ©Matt Berger/Shutterstock, cr ©Jan Martin Will/Shutterstock; p. 36 all ©istockphoto; p. 37 all ©istockphoto; p. 38 ©istockphoto; p. 39 all ©istockphoto; p. 41 ©istockphoto; p. 43 ©istockphoto.

Copyright ©2015 by Rand McNally

All rights reserved. No part of this work may be reproduced or transmitted in any form or by any means electronic or mechanical, including photocopying and recording, or by any information storage or retrieval system except by permission of the publisher.

Manufactured by Rand McNally
Skokie, Illinois 60077

Printed in Madison, WI, U.S.A.
August 2015
1st Printing
PO# 40604
ISBN 0-528-01507-9
ISBN-13: 978-0-528-01507-6

For information about ordering the *Junior Classroom Atlas* or the *Junior Classroom Atlas Teacher's Guide*, call 1-800-333-0136 or visit our website at www.randmcnally.com/education.

Table of Contents

Maps and Globes

Maps and globes help people learn about the earth.
A **globe** is a model of the earth.
A **map** is a drawing of the earth's surface.

Earth from space

The earth is shaped like a **sphere**, or ball. This picture taken from space shows some of the earth's land and water through clouds.

Water covers about three-fourths of the earth's surface. From space the earth looks blue.

Did You Know?

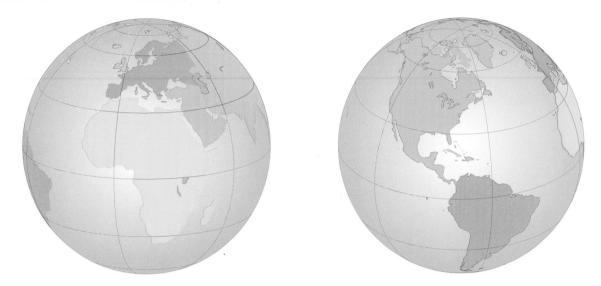

A globe is shaped like the earth. When you turn the globe, you see a different part of the earth.

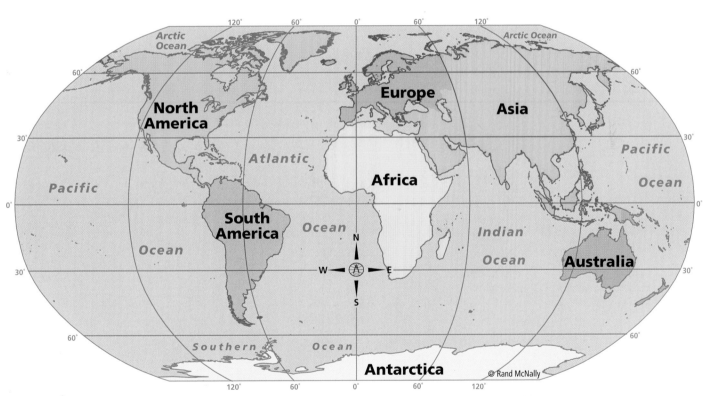

A map is flat. It can show all of the earth's surface at once.

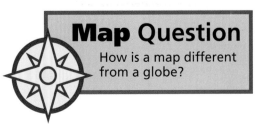

Map Question

How is a map different from a globe?

The World's Land and Water

The world is made up of land and water. **Continents** are the largest bodies of land. **Oceans** are the largest bodies of water.

World Physical Map

———	Country boundary
⌒	River
(shaded)	Mountains
Europe	Continent
Atlantic Ocean	Ocean
▪ London	Major city

Land Elevation
- 10,000 feet and over
- 5,000 – 10,000 feet
- 2,000 – 5,000 feet
- 1,000 – 2,000 feet
- 500 – 1,000 feet
- 0 – 500 feet

Water Depth
- Less than 600 feet
- 600 – 6,500 feet
- More than 6,500 feet

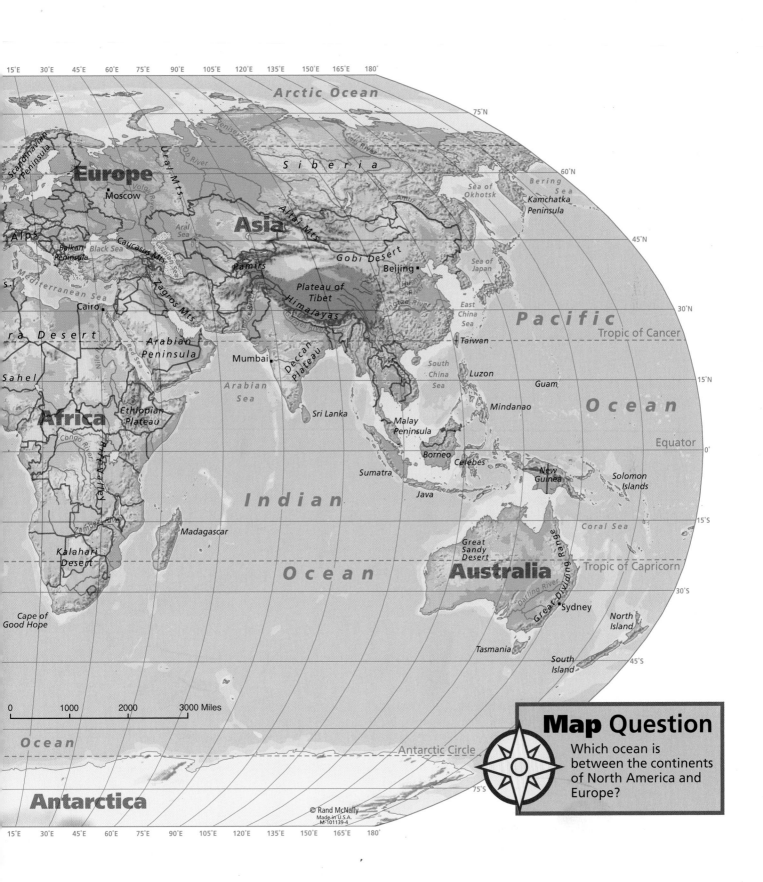

Arctic Ocean

75°N

60°N

Europe

Scandinavian Peninsula

•Moscow

Ural Mts.

Ob River

Yenisey River

Lena River

S i b e r i a

Bering Sea

75°N

60°N

45°N

30°N

Alps

Balkan Peninsula

Black Sea

Caucasus Mts.

Aral Sea

Asia

Altai Mts.

Sea of Okhotsk

Kamchatka Peninsula

Volga River

Mediterranean Sea

Zagros Mts.

Pamirs

Gobi Desert

Beijing•

Huang River

Sea of Japan

45°N

s.

Cairo•

Plateau of Tibet

Himalayas

Ganges River

Yangtze River

East China Sea

P a c i f i c

30°N

ra Desert

Arabian Peninsula

Red Sea

Mumbai•

Deccan Plateau

Taiwan•

Tropic of Cancer

S a h e l

Arabian Sea

Sri Lanka

South China Sea

Luzon

Guam•

O c e a n

15°N

Africa

Ethiopian Plateau

Malay Peninsula

Mindanao

Congo River

Nile River

Rift Valley

Borneo

Celebes

New Guinea

Solomon Islands

Equator

0°

Sumatra

Java

I n d i a n

Zambezi River

Madagascar

Coral Sea

15°S

Kalahari Desert

Great Sandy Desert

Australia

Great Dividing Range

Tropic of Capricorn

O c e a n

30°S

Cape of Good Hope

Darling River

Sydney•

North Island

Tasmania

South Island

45°S

| 0 | 1000 | 2000 | 3000 Miles |

O c e a n

Antarctic Circle

75°S

Antarctica

© Rand McNally
Made in U.S.A.
M-101139-4

15°E 30°E 45°E 60°E 75°E 90°E 105°E 120°E 135°E 150°E 165°E 180°

15°E 30°E 45°E 60°E 75°E 90°E 105°E 120°E 135°E 150°E 165°E 180°

Map Question

Which ocean is between the continents of North America and Europe?

7

The World's Countries

The world's continents are divided into **countries**.
A **country boundary** shows where a country begins and ends.

World Political Map

———	Country boundary
⌒	River
▨	Mountains
Asia	Continent
United States	Country
★ Ottawa	Country capital
Indian Ocean	Ocean

Map Question

Trace the country boundaries of the United States.

What countries does the United States touch?

World Land Use

People use the world's land in different ways. Many people in cities earn a living by **manufacturing**, or making goods.

Forestry in North America

Trees from North America's forests provide such things as lumber for building houses and pulp for making paper.

Trade in Europe

Europe has many busy ports where ships load and unload goods from around the world.

Herding in South America

Herders in some parts of South America raise llamas. These animals provide wool and transportation.

Farming in Asia

Rice is the most important crop grown in Asia. It can be grown on flat land or even on steep hillsides.

World Land Use

- Little or no use
- Herding, hunting, small farming
- Forestry
- Farming
- Ranching
- Manufacturing, trade
- Fishing

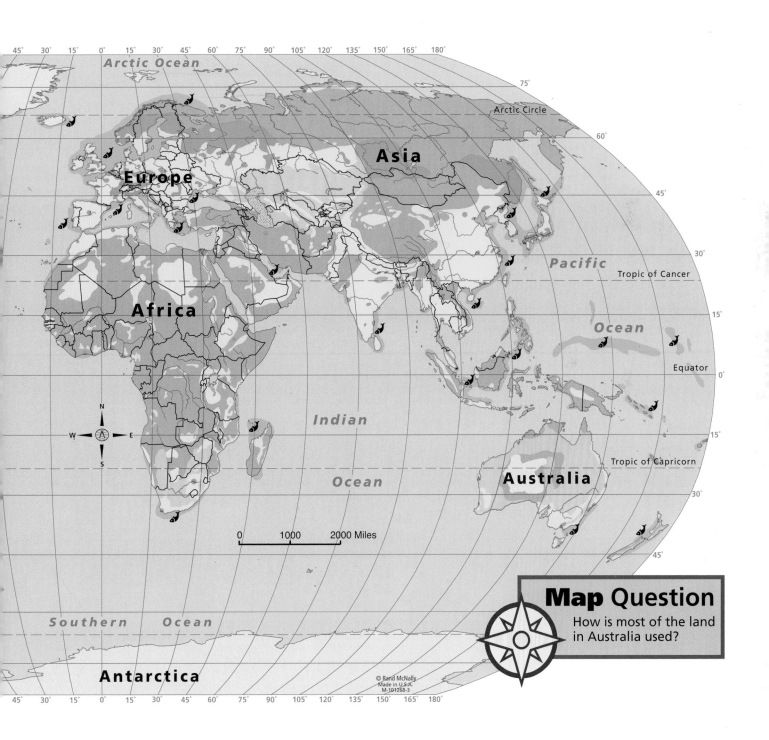

Map Question

How is most of the land in Australia used?

World Climate

Climate is how hot or cold, wet or dry a place is.
Some places have a climate that changes with the seasons.

Cross-country skiing in Canada
Parts of Canada have long, cold winters and short, cool summers.

Rain forest in Brazil
Rain forests receive more than 80 inches of rain a year. Many of the world's rain forests are near the equator.

Olive groves in Spain
Parts of Spain have hot, dry summers and rainy winters.

Farming in Indonesia
Rice grows well in places that are hot and rainy all year.

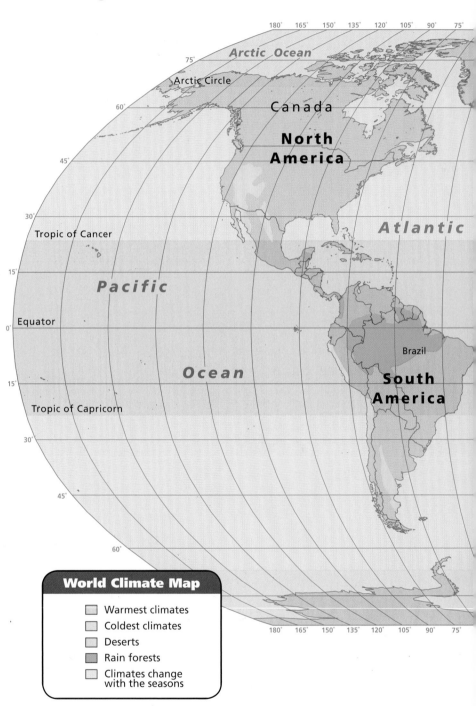

World Climate Map
- ☐ Warmest climates
- ☐ Coldest climates
- ☐ Deserts
- ☐ Rain forests
- ☐ Climates change with the seasons

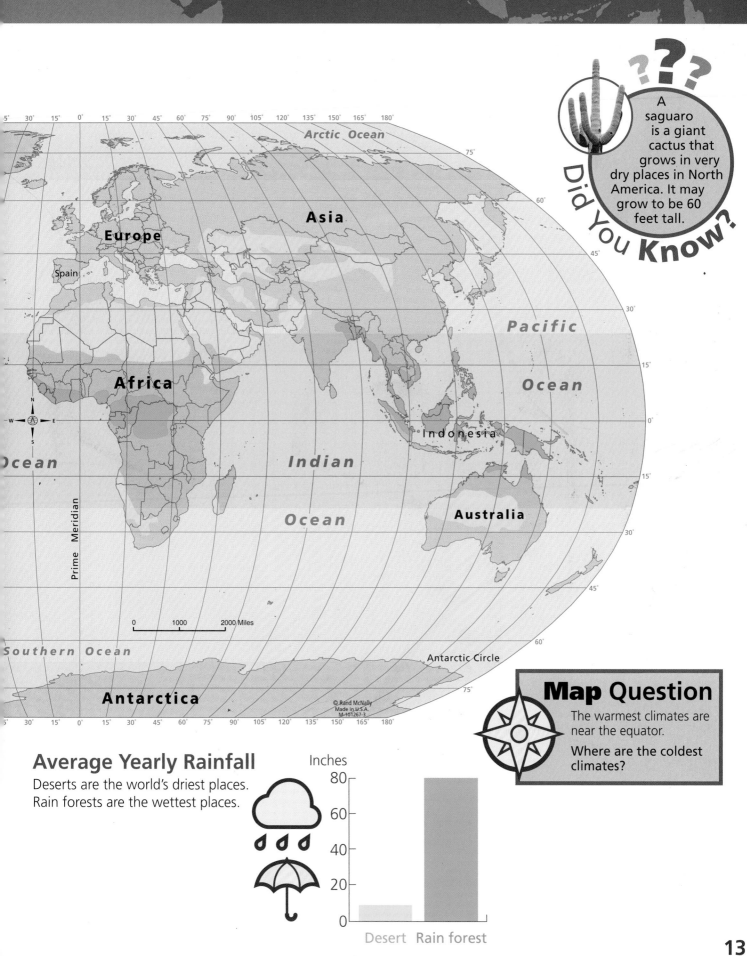

A saguaro is a giant cactus that grows in very dry places in North America. It may grow to be 60 feet tall.

Did You Know?

Map Question

The warmest climates are near the equator.

Where are the coldest climates?

Average Yearly Rainfall

Deserts are the world's driest places. Rain forests are the wettest places.

Inches

80

60

40

20

0

Desert   Rain forest

13

United States

The **United States** is made up of fifty states.
Each state has a **state capital**, which is a city where state government leaders work.

Map Question

What city is the capital of your state?

14

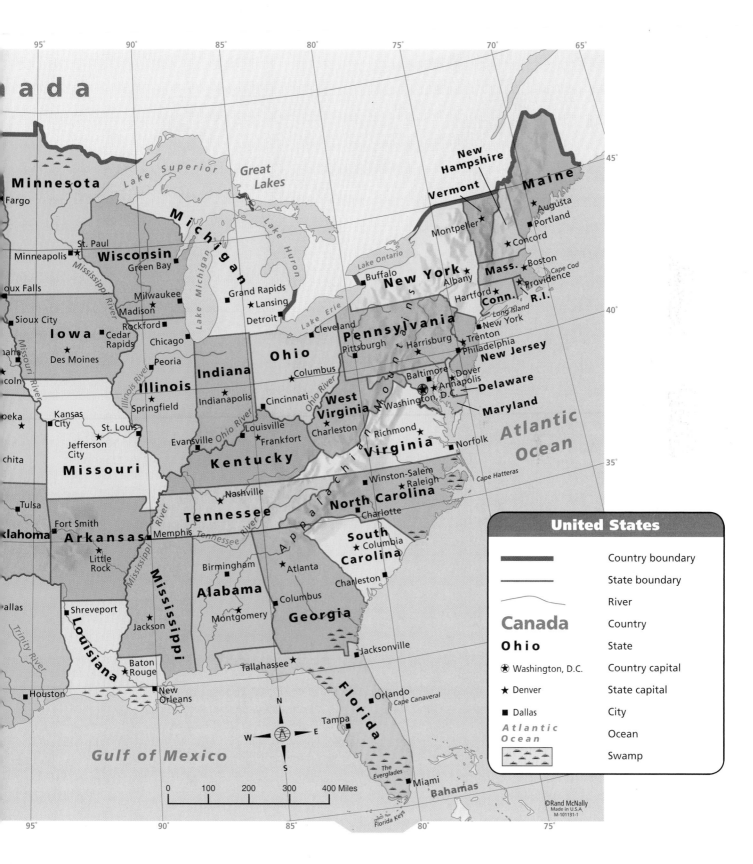

Canada

Minnesota

Fargo

Lake Superior

Great Lakes

Lake Michigan

Michigan

Lake Huron

New Hampshire

Vermont

Maine

Augusta

Portland

Montpelier

Concord

St. Paul

Minneapolis

Wisconsin

Green Bay

Milwaukee

Madison

Rockford

Sioux Falls

Mississippi River

Sioux City

Iowa

Cedar Rapids

Chicago

Peoria

Des Moines

Lincoln

Illinois River

Illinois

Springfield

Indiana

Indianapolis

Ohio

Columbus

Cincinnati

Lake Erie

Cleveland

Buffalo

New York

Albany

Lake Ontario

Pennsylvania

Pittsburgh

Harrisburg

Mass.

Boston

Cape Cod

Providence

Conn.

Hartford

R.I.

Long Island

New York

Trenton

Philadelphia

New Jersey

Dover

Delaware

Baltimore

Annapolis

Washington, D.C.

Maryland

Topeka

Kansas City

St. Louis

West Virginia

Louisville

Frankfort

Charleston

Evansville

Ohio River

Kentucky

Richmond

Virginia

Norfolk

Atlantic Ocean

Jefferson City

Missouri

Wichita

Tulsa

Nashville

Tennessee

Memphis

Tennessee River

Winston-Salem

Raleigh

North Carolina

Charlotte

Cape Hatteras

Oklahoma

Fort Smith

Arkansas

Little Rock

Mississippi River

Mississippi

Birmingham

Atlanta

South Carolina

Columbia

Charleston

Dallas

Shreveport

Louisiana

Jackson

Alabama

Montgomery

Columbus

Georgia

Jacksonville

Trinity River

Houston

Baton Rouge

New Orleans

Tallahassee

Florida

Orlando

Cape Canaveral

Tampa

N
W · E
S

Gulf of Mexico

The Everglades

Miami

Bahamas

Florida Keys

0 100 200 300 400 Miles

©Rand McNally
Made in U.S.A.
M-101131-1

United States

———	Country boundary
———	State boundary
⌒	River
Canada	Country
Ohio	State
✪ Washington, D.C.	Country capital
★ Denver	State capital
■ Dallas	City
Atlantic Ocean	Ocean
▦	Swamp

15

United States Regions

The United States can be divided into regions in many different ways. This map shows one way.

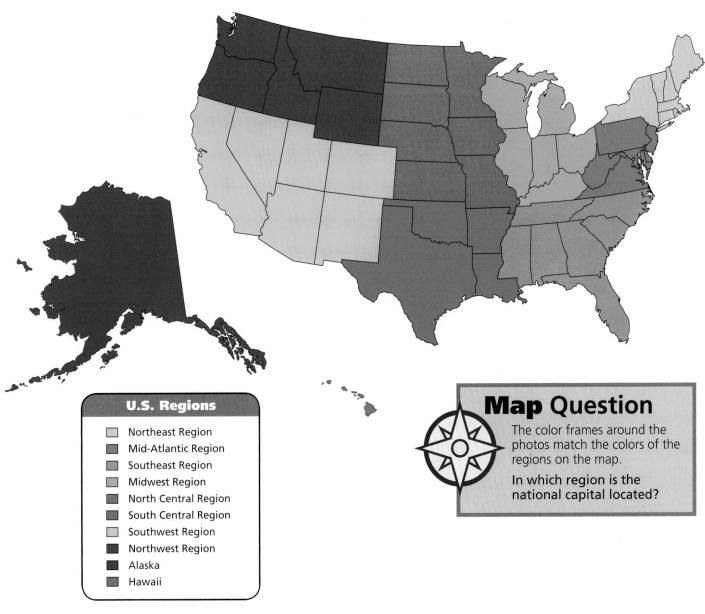

U.S. Regions

- Northeast Region
- Mid-Atlantic Region
- Southeast Region
- Midwest Region
- North Central Region
- South Central Region
- Southwest Region
- Northwest Region
- Alaska
- Hawaii

Map Question

The color frames around the photos match the colors of the regions on the map.

In which region is the national capital located?

The United States through History

About 1,200 years ago
The Hohokam farmed in the desert Southwest.

About 800 years ago
The Anasazi built cliff dwellings in the Southwest.

| 900 A.D | 1000 A.D. | 1100 | 1200 | 1300 | 1400 |

About 1,000 years ago
Vikings from Greenland explored the northeast coast of North America.

Fall in Maine

The United States Capitol building in Washington, D.C.

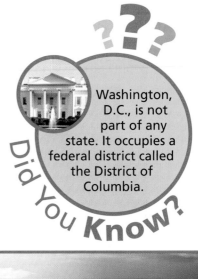
Did You Know?
Washington, D.C., is not part of any state. It occupies a federal district called the District of Columbia.

The Outer Banks of North Carolina

Farms in Wisconsin

Badlands of South Dakota

A bayou in Louisiana

The Grand Canyon in Arizona

Seattle, Washington

About 500 years ago
Spanish explorers traveled through the south and southwestern parts of what is now the United States.

A little more than 200 years ago
The colonies won freedom from Great Britain, and the United States became a nation.

| 1500 | 1600 | 1700 | 1800 | 1900 | 2000 |

About 400 years ago
English settlers started colonies along the Atlantic Coast.

About 100 years ago
Millions of European immigrants settled in the United States.

17

South America

South America has thirteen mainland countries.
All but two of them are located along a coast.

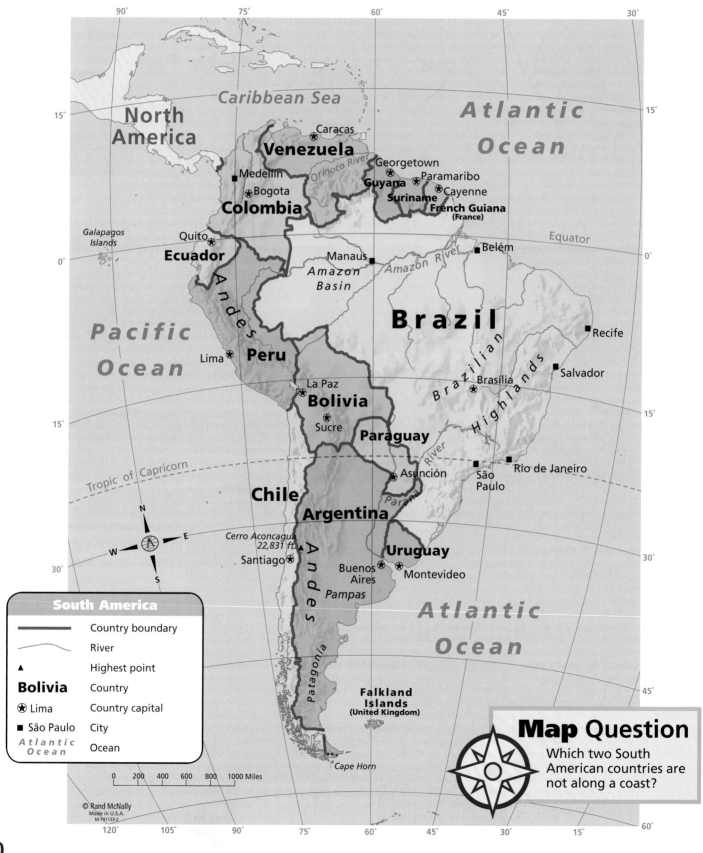

South America

———	Country boundary
⌒	River
▲	Highest point
Bolivia	Country
✪ Lima	Country capital
■ São Paulo	City
Atlantic Ocean	Ocean

0   200   400   600   800   1000 Miles

© Rand McNally
Made in U.S.A.
M-101133-2

Map Question
Which two South American countries are not along a coast?

???

Did You Know?

The giant tortoises of the Galapagos Islands can live for more than 140 years.

That's a Lot of Coffee!

Brazil and Colombia produce more coffee beans than any other countries in the world.

Brazil   〇〇〇〇〇〇〇〇〇〇〇〇〇〇〇〇〇〇

Columbia   〇〇〇〇〇〇〇

Indonesia   〇〇〇〇〇

Vietnam   〇〇〇〇

Each 〇 = 100,000 tons of coffee beans

Amazon rain forest in Brazil

The world's largest tropical rain forest covers most of northern South America.

Machu Picchu in Peru

The stone ruins of this ancient Inca city are high in the Andes Mountains.

Outdoor market in Bolivia

Indians from villages in the Andes gather to buy and sell goods.

— South America through History —

About 600 years ago
The Inca ruled lands along the west coast of South America.

About 400 years ago
Spain ruled much of South America.

About 100 years ago
One million people lived in Buenos Aires, Argentina.

| 1400 | 1500 | 1600 | 1700 | 1800 | 1900 | 2000 |

About 500 years ago
Portugal claimed Brazil.

About 200 years ago
South American countries won their freedom from European rulers.

21

Europe

Europe is a small continent, but it has many people. It has some of the world's most famous cities.

45°   60°   75°

60°

Map Question

Moscow is Europe's largest city.

In what country is it located?

R u s s i a

Perm ■

75°

Ural Mountains

A s i a

Volga River

Kama River

⊛ Moscow

45°

K a z a k h s t a n

Kiev

Volgograd ■

Volga River

Ukraine

60°

Caspian Sea

Caucasus Mts.
▲ Mt. Elbrus
18,510 ft.

Azerbaijan

Black Sea

Istanbul

Europe	
————	Country boundary
⌒	River
▲	Highest point
Spain	Country
⊛ Paris	Country capital
■ Munich	City
Atlantic Ocean	Ocean

r k e y

30°

A s i a

0 100 200 300 400 Miles

© Rand McNally
Made in U.S.A.
M-101134-3

Sea

30°   45°

23

The Parthenon in Athens, Greece
This ancient temple was built by the Greeks to honor the goddess Athena.

The Eiffel Tower in Paris, France
The Eiffel Tower is a popular place for tourists to visit. They can go to the top of the 984-foot tower for a view of Paris.

The Colosseum in Rome, Italy
This large outdoor amphitheater was built by the Romans almost 2,000 years ago.

Tower of Big Ben in London, England
Big Ben is a famous bell in the clock tower of the Houses of Parliament in London.

Europe through History

About 5,000 years ago
Minoan culture began on the island of Crete.

About 2,000 years ago
The Roman Empire ruled a huge area around the Mediterranean Sea.

About 700 years ago
The Renaissance brought new interest in art and science.

3000 B.C.	2000 B.C.	1000 B.C.	1000 A.D.	1100	1200	1300

About 4,500 years ago
Greek civilization began.

About 1,000 years ago
Towns began to grow in Europe.

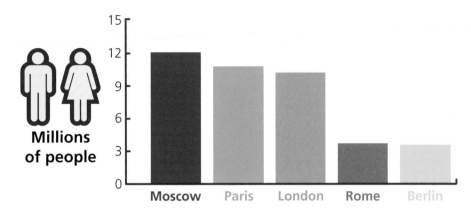

Did You Know?

The Matterhorn is one of the most famous mountains in the world.

How many people?

This graph compares the populations of five of Europe's largest cities.

Millions of people

15	

Moscow · Paris · London · Rome · Berlin

Basketmaker in Scotland
Europe has many factories, but some workers make goods by hand.

High-speed train in France
Express trains carry passengers to major cities throughout Europe.

Skiing in the Alps
Winter sports are popular in many parts of Europe.

About 500 years ago
Europeans began to explore the world.

About 200 years ago
European nations set up colonies in Africa and Asia.

1400 · 1500 · 1600 · 1700 · 1800 · 1900 · 2000

About 300 years ago
The Industrial Revolution brought many new ways of making goods.

About 70 years ago
Many European cities were destroyed in World War II.

25

Africa

Africa has both rain forests and deserts. The Sahara is the largest desert in the world. It covers most of the northern part of the continent.

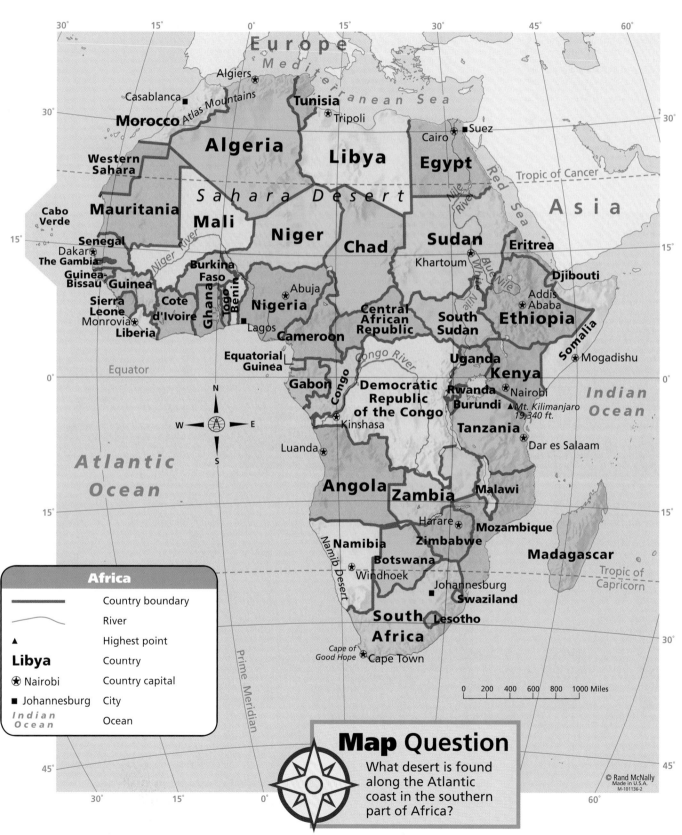

Africa

————	Country boundary
∿	River
▲	Highest point
Libya	Country
✪ Nairobi	Country capital
■ Johannesburg	City
Indian Ocean	Ocean

Map Question

What desert is found along the Atlantic coast in the southern part of Africa?

© Rand McNally
Made in U.S.A.
M-101136-2

The Longest River on Each Continent

The Nile River in Africa is the longest river in the world.

Nile (Africa) — 4,145 miles

Amazon (South America) — 4,000 miles

Yangtze (Asia) — 3,900 miles

Mississippi-Missouri (North America) — 3,740 miles

Murray-Darling (Australia) — 2,330 miles

Volga (Europe) — 2,194 miles

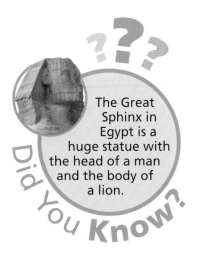

Did You Know?

The Great Sphinx in Egypt is a huge statue with the head of a man and the body of a lion.

Ancient statues in Egypt
These giant statues were carved thousands of years ago. They were part of a temple honoring an Egyptian king.

Lowland gorillas in central Africa
Lowland gorillas live in rain forests near the equator.

Modern buildings in Johannesburg, South Africa
Johannesburg is the largest city in South Africa. It is one of Africa's most important trade centers.

Africa through History

About 5,100 years ago
Egypt became a great kingdom.

About 600 years ago
Powerful kingdoms began in central and southern Africa.

About 100 years ago
European countries ruled most of Africa.

| 3000 B.C. | 1000 B.C. | 1400 A.D. | 1600 | 1800 | 2000 |

About 4,000 years ago
The kingdom of Kush became a center of art, learning, and trade.

About 500 years ago
Portuguese explorers sailed around Africa to India.

About 60 years ago
African countries began to win freedom from European rule.

27

Asia

Asia is the largest continent. It has more land and more people than any other continent.

Arctic Ocean

Europe

* Moscow

Russia

Ural Mountains

Ob River

Sib

Omsk

Novosibirsk

Astana

Kazakhstan

Mongol

Black Sea

Ankara

Turkey

Georgia

Armenia

Azerbaijan

Caspian Sea

Cyprus

Uzbekistan

Lebanon
Israel

Syria

Tigris River

Turkmenistan

Kyrgyzstan

Jerusalem

Iraq

Baghdad

Tajikistan

Egypt

Jordan

Euphrates River

Tehran

Iran

Kabul

Indus River

Kyrgyzstan

China

Kuwait

Afghanistan

Islamabad

Himalayas

Mediterranean Sea

Tropic of Cancer

Africa

Riyadh

Bahrain

Mecca

Qatar

Pakistan

New
Delhi

Nepal

Bhutan

Saudi
Arabia

U.A.E.

Mt. Everest
29,028 ft.

Red Sea

Muscat

Karachi

Ganges River

Bangladesh

Sanaa

Yemen

Oman

Mumbai

India

Kolkata

Ayeyarwady River

Myanmar
(Burma)

Arabian

Rangoon

Sea

Bay of
Bengal

Bangko

Bengaluru

Chennai

Sri Lanka

Equator

Indian Ocean

Asia

———	Country boundary
~~	River
▲	Highest point
China	Country
✪ Tehran	Country capital
■ Mumbai	City
Pacific Ocean	Ocean

N
W   E
S

0 200 400 600 800 1000 Miles

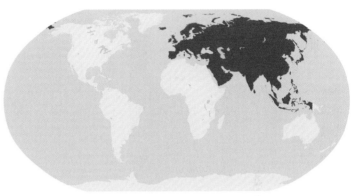

Eurasia
The continents of Europe and Asia form one large body of land called Eurasia.

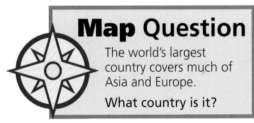

Map Question

The world's largest country covers much of Asia and Europe.

What country is it?

Asia

Farming in India
Some farmers in Asia use animals to pull plows.

Transportation in China
Many people use bicycles to get around in China's crowded cities.

Oil refinery in Southwest Asia
Much of the world's oil comes from countries in Southwest Asia.

Hong Kong Harbor
Hong Kong is one of the most important port cities in Asia.

The Himalayas in Nepal
The Himalayas are the highest mountains in the world. Their name means "House of Snow."

Ancient ruins in Turkey
Turkey is the westernmost country in Asia.

Asia through History

About 11,000 years ago
People began farming in Southwest Asia.

About 2,200 years ago
China began building the Great Wall.

9000 B.C.	7000 B.C.	5000 B.C.	3000 B.C.	1000 B.C.	1000 A.D.

About 5,500 years ago
Civilization began between the Tigris and Euphrates Rivers.

About 1,900 years ago
The Chinese invented paper.

Giant pandas live in China's bamboo forests. They weigh up to 350 pounds.

Did You Know?

World Population

Asia has more people than all the other continents added together.

Australia
South America
North America
Europe
Asia
Africa

The Taj Mahal in India
An Indian ruler built the Taj Mahal in memory of his wife. The beautiful building is made of white marble.

Skyscrapers in Tokyo, Japan
Tokyo is the capital of Japan. It is the largest city in the world.

The Great Wall of China
The Chinese built the Great Wall to protect their country. It is about 25 feet high and 4,600 miles long.

About 400 years ago
The Taj Mahal was built in India.

About 60 years ago
India and other Asian nations won freedom.

| 1200 | 1400 | 1600 | 1800 | 2000 |

About 200 years ago
European nations controlled parts of Asia.

31

Australia

Australia is both a continent and a country. It is the world's smallest continent, but it is the sixth-largest country.

Australia (legend)

‿‿‿	River
▲	Highest point
Australia	Country
✪ Canberra	Country capital
■ Melbourne	City
Pacific Ocean	Ocean

Map Question

What is the only country capital on the continent of Australia?

A kangaroo can hop as fast as 30 miles per hour. It can jump six feet high.

Did You Know?

Leading Sheep-Raising Countries

Australia is the world's leading producer of sheep and wool.

Australia
China
New Zealand
Iran
India

Each = 10 million sheep

Uluru, near Alice Springs

Uluru is also called Ayers Rock. It has many caves with paintings made by people who lived there long ago.

Sydney Opera House and skyline

Sydney is the largest city in Australia. The Sydney Opera House is the city's most famous landmark.

The Great Barrier Reef

Divers can see many kinds of fish and coral along the Great Barrier Reef. The reef stretches for more than 1,200 miles along the northeast coast of Australia.

Australia through History

About 600 years ago
Chinese settlers arrived in northern Australia.

About 200 years ago
Great Britain began to claim land in Australia.

About 100 years ago
Australia became a nation.

| 1400 | 1500 | 1600 | 1700 | 1800 | 1900 | 2000 |

About 400 years ago
Dutch sailors explored the coasts of Australia.

About 150 years ago
Gold was discovered in Australia.

33

Antarctica

Antarctica is the coldest continent. A thick layer of ice and snow covers most of the land.

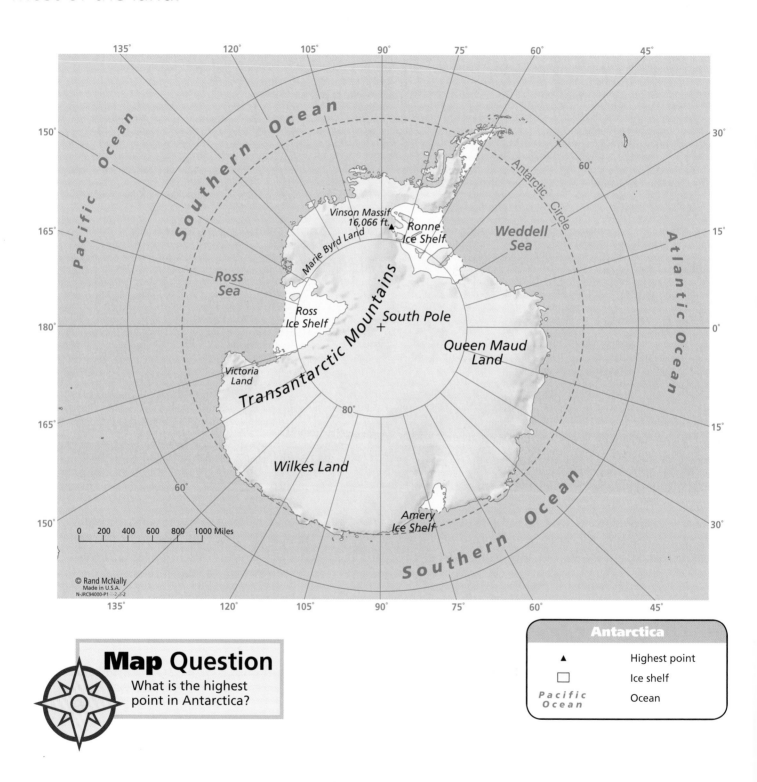

Map Question

What is the highest point in Antarctica?

Antarctica	
▲	Highest point
□	Ice shelf
Pacific Ocean	Ocean

Lowest Recorded Temperature on Each Continent

Antarctica is the coldest place in the world.

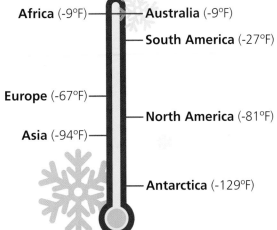

Africa (-9°F) — Australia (-9°F)
South America (-27°F)
Europe (-67°F)
North America (-81°F)
Asia (-94°F)
Antarctica (-129°F)

??? Did You Know?

The highest temperature ever recorded in Antarctica is 59° F.

Emperor penguins

Emperor penguins live in large colonies on the sea ice along Antarctica's coast.

Antarctic iceberg

As temperatures get warmer in summer, pieces break off Antarctica's ice shelves. The pieces can form huge icebergs.

Scientists in Antarctica

Scientists study Antarctica during the summer. Very few people stay on this cold, barren continent during the winter.

Antarctica through History

About 200 years ago
Explorers first sighted Antarctica.

About 50 years ago
Twelve countries agreed to use Antarctica only for scientific research.

1700 — 1800 — 1900 — 2000

About 100 years ago
A Norwegian explorer reached the South Pole.

35

Handbook of Map Skills

Geographical Terms

This drawing shows many features of the earth. To find the meanings of some of the terms, look in the word list below.

Canyon: A deep, narrow valley with high, steep sides

Cape: A narrow piece of land that extends into the sea

Coast: Land along a large lake, sea, or ocean

Desert: A large land area that receives little rainfall

Forest: A large land area covered with trees

Gulf: A large area of water within a curved coastline; a gulf is larger than a bay and smaller than a sea

Harbor: A protected body of water where ships can anchor safely

Hill: A small land area higher than the land around it

Island: A piece of land surrounded by water

Lake: An inland body of water

Mountain: Land that rises much higher than the land around it

Peninsula: A piece of land nearly surrounded by water

Plain: A large, flat land area

Plateau: A large, high land area that is generally flat

River: A body of fresh water that flows from higher to lower land

Sea: A large body of salt water partly surrounded by land

Valley: The lower land between hills or mountains

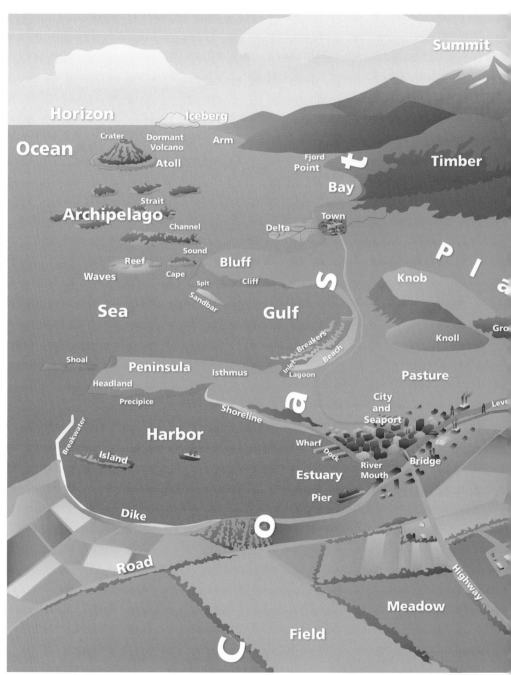

Coast

Desert

Forest

Peak

Glacier · Snow Line · Pass · **Mountain Range** · Active Volcano

Timberline · Foothills · Gulch · Hill · Cinder Cone

Canyon · Tableland · Village · **P i e d m o n t** · Divide

Plateau · Brink · Reservoir

Forest · Valley · Stream · Waterfall · Chasm

Brook · Rapids · Dam · Power Plant · Tunnel

Lake · Marsh · **R I D G E** · Canal · Irrigated Land

iver · Bayou · Branch · **Woods** · **Oasis**

Railroad · Right Bank · Locks · **Gorge** · Dune

Left Bank · Mesa

Cultivated Land · Crag

Airport · **S l o p e** · Pond · Ledge

Desert

Harbor · Island · Mountain · Valley

North America

Caribbean Sea

Atlantic Ocean

Caracas

Venezuela

Medellín

Orinoco River

Georgetown

Paramaribo

Guyana

Cayenne

Suriname

Bogota

French Guiana
(France)

Colombia

Galapagos Islands

Quito

Ecuador

Equator

Belém

Manaus

Amazon Basin

Amazon River

Pacific Ocean

Andes

B r a z i l

Recife

Lima

Peru

Brazilian

La Paz

Brasília

Salvador

Bolivia

Highlands

Sucre

Paraguay

River

Rio de Janeiro

Tropic of Capricorn

Asunción

São Paulo

N
E
W
S

Chile

Argentina

Paraná

Cerro Aconcagua
22,831 ft.

Uruguay

Andes

Santiago

Buenos Aires

Montevideo

Pampas

Atlantic Ocean

Patagonia

0 200 400 600 800 1000 Miles

Falkland Islands
(United Kingdom)

Cape Horn

© Rand McNally
Made in U.S.A.
M-101133-2

Map Question

What symbol on the map stands for a river?

Symbols

Symbols are lines, colors, and shapes that stand for something else. Maps use symbols to stand for real places on the earth.

Ocean

River

City

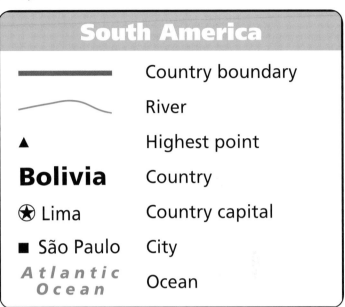
Mountains

Legend

A **map legend** explains what the symbols on a map mean.

South America

———	Country boundary
∿	River
▲	Highest point
Bolivia	Country
★ Lima	Country capital
■ São Paulo	City
Atlantic Ocean	Ocean

Compass Rose

A **compass rose** shows directions on a map. The letters stand for **N**orth, **E**ast, **S**outh, and **W**est.

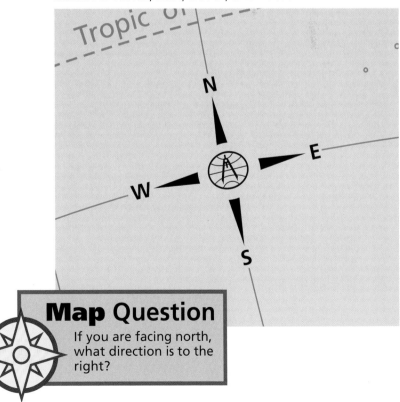
Tropic of

N
E
W
S

Map Question

If you are facing north, what direction is to the right?

Handbook of Map Skills

Bar Scale
A **bar scale** helps you understand distances on a map.

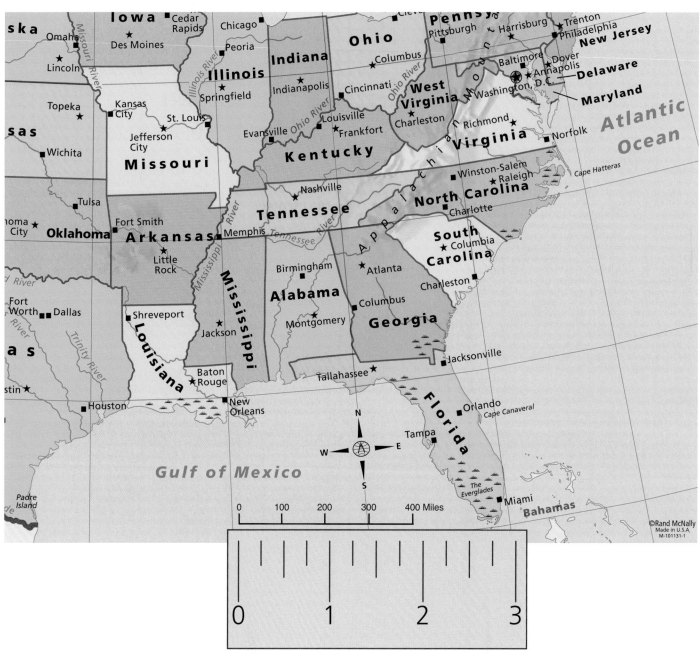

Place a ruler next to the bar scale on this map.
You will see that one inch on the map is equal to
a little more than 200 miles on the earth.

A bar scale helps you measure distances on a map.
Copy the bar scale onto a strip of paper.

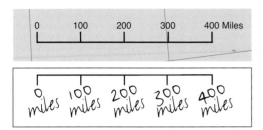

Use your paper bar scale to find distances on the map.

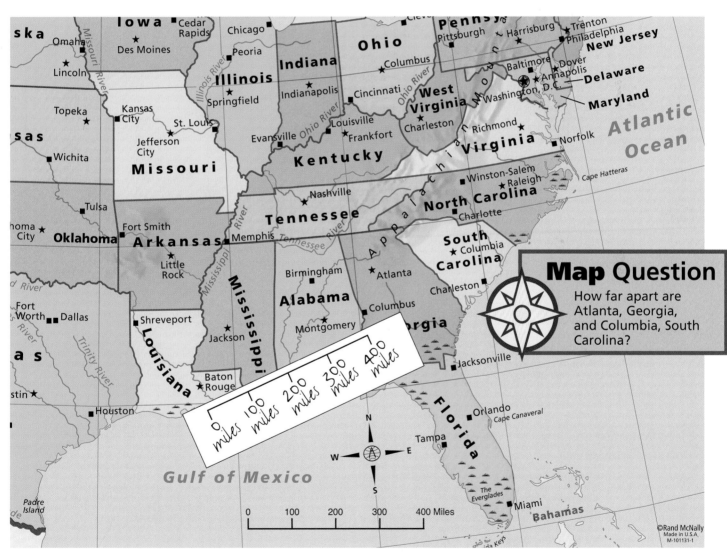

Map Question

How far apart are Atlanta, Georgia, and Columbia, South Carolina?

Baton Rouge, Louisiana, and Montgomery, Alabama, are a little more than 300 miles apart.

Handbook of Map Skills

Latitude

Latitude lines run east and west on globes and maps.

The **Equator** is a latitude line that divides the earth in half. It represents 0 degrees latitude.

All other latitude lines are numbered based upon their distance from the equator.

Each half of the earth is call a **hemisphere**.

All land and water north of the Equator is in the
Northern Hemisphere.

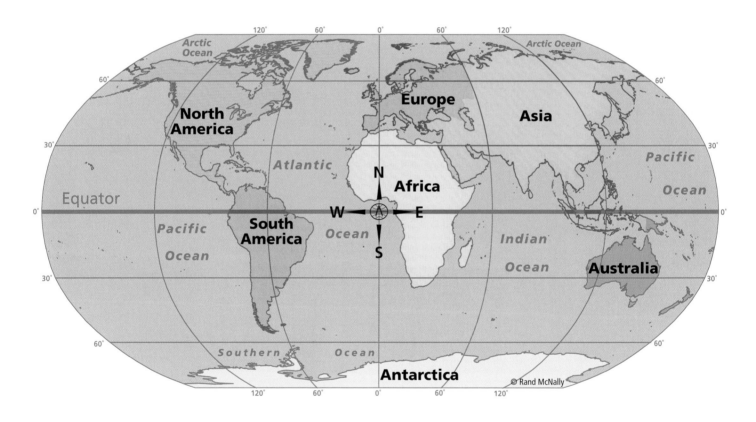

All land and water south of the Equator is in the
Southern Hemisphere.

Longitude

Longitude lines run north and south from pole to pole on globes and maps.

The **Prime Meridian** is the longitude line that represents 0 degrees of longitude.

All other longitude lines are numbered based upon their distance from the Prime Meridian.

Each half of the earth is called a **hemisphere**.

All land and water west of the Prime Meridian is in the **Western Hemisphere**.

All land and water east of the Prime Meridian is in the **Eastern Hemisphere**.

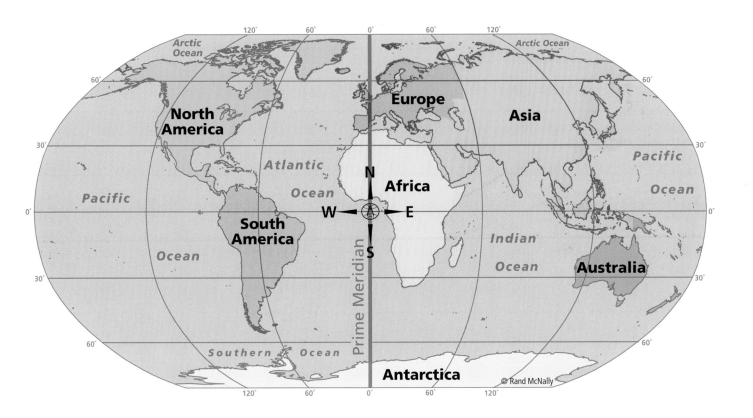

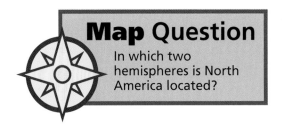

Map Question

In which two hemispheres is North America located?

43

Glossary

bar scale	the part of a map that helps you measure distances; the bar scale tells how many miles on the earth's surface are shown by each inch on the map
climate	how hot or cold, wet or dry a place is over a long period of time
compass rose	the part of a map that shows directions; the letters on a compass rose stand for North, East, South, and West
continent	one of the seven largest bodies of land on the earth
country	a land that has a government
country boundary	a line on a map that shows where a country begins and ends
Eastern Hemisphere	all land and water on the earth east of the Prime Meridian
Equator	the latitude line that divides the earth into the Northern Hemisphere and the Southern Hemisphere
globe	a model of the earth
hemisphere	half of the earth
latitude lines	lines that run east and west on a globe or a map
longitude lines	lines that run north and south on a globe or a map
manufacturing	making goods

map legend	the part of a map that explains what the symbols on the map mean
map	a drawing of the earth's surface
national capital	a city where a nation's government leaders work
Northern Hemisphere	all land and water on the earth north of the Equator
ocean	one of the five largest bodies of salt water on the earth
Prime Meridian	the longitude line that divides the earth into the Eastern Hemisphere and the Western Hemisphere
regions	places that have something in common
Southern Hemisphere	all land and water on the earth south of the Equator
sphere	a ball; the earth is shaped like a sphere
state	part of a country; the United States is a country with fifty states
state boundary	a line on a map that shows where a state begins and ends
state capital	a city where state government leaders work
symbols	lines, colors, and shapes that stand for something else
Western Hemisphere	all land and water on the earth west of the Prime Meridian

Index

Index Abbreviations

Index